Life Cycle of a Salmon

by Meg Gaertner

FOCUS READERS®

PIONEER

www.focusreaders.com

Focus Readers is distributed by North Star Editions:
sales@northstareditions.com | 888-417-0195

Produced for Focus Readers by Red Line Editorial.

Photographs ©: iStockphoto, cover, 1, 12, 15, 17; Shutterstock Images, 4, 7, 8, 11, 18, 21 (fish), 21 (arrows)

Library of Congress Cataloging-in-Publication Data
Names: Gaertner, Meg, author.
Title: Life cycle of a salmon / by Meg Gaertner.
Description: Lake Elmo, MN : Focus Readers, [2022] | Series: Life
    cycles | Includes index. | Audience: Grades 2-3
Identifiers: LCCN 2021007320 (print) | LCCN 2021007321 (ebook) | ISBN
    9781644938324 (hardcover) | ISBN 9781644938782 (paperback) | ISBN
    9781644939246 (ebook) | ISBN 9781644939680 (pdf)
Subjects: LCSH: Salmon--Life cycles--Juvenile literature.
Classification: LCC QL638.S2 G34 2022 (print) | LCC QL638.S2 (ebook) |
    DDC 597.5/6156--dc23
LC record available at https://lccn.loc.gov/2021007320
LC ebook record available at https://lccn.loc.gov/2021007321

Printed in the United States of America
Mankato, MN
082021

About the Author

Meg Gaertner enjoys reading, writing, dancing, and being outside. She lives in Minnesota.

Table of Contents

Chapter 1

Egg

It is winter. **Female** salmon build nests at the bottoms of streams. Then they lay thousands of eggs. **Male** salmon **fertilize** the eggs.

The eggs are the size of peas. They fall into the nests. Female salmon cover the eggs with sand and small rocks. Then the adult salmon leave.

Fun Fact Female salmon use their tails to dig nests. They also use their tails to hide the eggs.

egg

Chapter 2

Alevin

Each egg has an **embryo** inside. It also has a yolk sac. This sac has many **nutrients**. The embryo uses those nutrients to grow.

Spring comes. The eggs **hatch**. Baby salmon come out. They are called alevin. These tiny fish stay in the nest. They still have yolk sacs attached to them. But soon the nutrients are gone. Then the alevin must leave the nest and look for food.

Chapter 3

Fry

Young salmon swim around freely. They are called fry. They eat tiny creatures in the water. They grow bigger. Then they eat insects.

Some fry swim straight to the sea. Others stay in fresh water for years. But all fry will head toward the ocean. They swim through rivers and streams to get there.

A Long Trip

Sometimes, fry swim actively toward the ocean. Other times, they let the river carry them. Fry change along the way. Salt water is different from fresh water. So, fry must prepare. They eat a lot. They also spend time in the **estuary**. There, they become used to the salt water.

Chapter 4

Adult

Salmon live for years in the ocean. Some stay near the shore. Others head farther out to sea. They grow and become **mature** adults.

Then salmon return home. This is a long trip. It takes a lot of energy. Salmon jump up waterfalls. They swim up rivers. They swim against the water's flow. Then they reach the streams where they hatched. Female salmon build nests. They lay eggs. The life cycle begins again.

Life Cycle Stages

Adult Salmon

Egg

Alevin

Fry

The fish changes as it heads to salt water.

FOCUS ON
Salmon Life Cycles

Write your answers on a separate piece of paper.

1. Write a sentence describing what happens during a salmon's trip to the ocean.

2. Which stage of the life cycle do you find most interesting? Why?

3. What is the name for newly hatched salmon with yolk sacs attached to them?
   - A. fry
   - B. alevin
   - C. eggs

4. Why does the trip back to freshwater streams take so much energy?
   - A. Salmon can let the river carry them.
   - B. Salmon swim against the river's flow.
   - C. Salmon are not mature yet.

Answer key on page 24.

Glossary

embryo
A stage of growth that happens before birth or hatching.

estuary
The place where a river meets the ocean.

female
Able to have babies or lay eggs.

fertilize
To make something able to grow a new animal.

hatch
To break open so a young animal can come out.

male
Unable to have babies or lay eggs.

mature
Fully grown.

nutrients
Things that people, animals, and plants need to stay healthy.

To Learn More

BOOKS

Fishman, Jon M. *The Salmon's Journey*. Minneapolis: Lerner Publications, 2018.

Hansen, Grace. *Salmon Migration*. Minneapolis: Abdo Publishing, 2018.

NOTE TO EDUCATORS

Visit **www.focusreaders.com** to find lesson plans, activities, links, and other resources related to this title.

Index

Answer Key: **1.** Answers will vary; **2.** Answers will vary; **3.** B; **4.** B